HOW TO BE
A BEDROOM
GODDESS

RYLAND
PETERS
& SMALL

LONDON NEW YORK

HOW TO BE
A BEDROOM
GODDESS

SOPHIA MORTENSEN

illustrations by Des Taylor

Senior Designer **Paul Tilby**
Senior Editor **Miriam Hyslop**
Production **Simon Walsh**
Art Director **Anne-Marie Bulat**
Publishing Director **Alison Starling**

Illustrations **Des.Taylor@pvuk.com**

First published in the
United Kingdom in 2006
by Ryland Peters & Small
20–21 Jockey's Fields
London WC1R 4BW
www.rylandpeters.com

10 9 8 7 6 5 4 3 2 1

Text, design and illustrations
© Ryland Peters & Small 2006

ISBN-10: 1 84597 269 4
ISBN-13: 978 1 84597 269 1

A CIP record for this book is
available from the British Library.

Printed in China

CONTENTS

INTRODUCTION

The goddess is a potent mythological figure that has captivated our sensual imagination since earliest times. The first religions of which we have any account were based upon nature-worship, in which the female was respected as the most important creative force. Ancient peoples lived in close harmony with the cycles of nature and it was initially thought the female alone was responsible for the giving of new life. The Earth was venerated as Mother Provider, the physical manifestation of the Great Goddess. She was bountiful and yielding but could also be cruel and tempestuous. Inevitably, ancient peoples were mindful of the consequences that could befall them if they became disrespectful of nature.

In matriarchal societies, the presence of the goddess was woven into ideas of love and sexual pleasure and it was not until after 10,000 BC that the male role in procreation began to be understood. This had a dramatic effect as warrior tribes spread across the globe and patriarchy became dominant. Yet still, the idea of the goddess survived. In the ancient civilizations of Sumeria, Babylon, Egypt, Greece and Rome, she is found as Inanna, Cybele, Ereshkigal, Isis, Aphrodite, Circe, Demeter and Venus, to name but a few of her incarnations, and she is always associated with erotic love. With the advent of patriarchal religions, goddess culture was demonized. Whereas previously goddesses had represented the sacredness of sexuality, it was now regarded as evil to be aligned with nature and much darker mythologies about sin were created to keep human sexuality under control.

Yet even in the most repressive times, the idea of a goddess burst through into our collective consciousness, emerging in stories, paintings and myths to enchant us and remind us that the universal female energies cannot be denied, and that we must strive for harmony between male and female. The fascination with feminine beauty is timeless, and the primal drive for sexual union is hotwired into our biology. Although modern culture has a tendency to cheapen sex, erotic desire, when respected and channelled into life-enhancing relationships, is part of the wonderful, multi-faceted gift of life.

Men will always be drawn to women who exude the sexual magnetism of a goddess – something not necessarily reliant on age or dress size! This little book will show how you can tap into the natural love goddess within you, becoming a woman of mystery and sexual allure. You will learn sex tips from history, enjoying your unique feminine qualities with renewed interest as you discover just how sophisticated our ancestors were in their private bedchambers. The second part of the book is packed with ideas for the modern goddess, drawing on the secrets of priestesses and courtesans who were experts in the erotic arts and also in the ways of men. So get ready to stoke the fires of your imagination and see ecstatic results for you and your partner!

BEDROOM GODDESS THROUGH TIME

nature worship
& the great goddess

We cannot know exactly what our distant ancestors got up to in their caves, but we do know they were more sophisticated than the stereotype of hairy brutes with limited intelligence. The discovery of Palaeolithic sex toys – most likely used for ritual deflowering as a rite of passage – proves that our forebears had an imagination. We also know from cave paintings and early carvings that fertility was prized, and both the pregnant woman and the erect male were revered as symbols of potency, charged with the life force.

Early peoples were immersed in the phenomenon of being alive and magic was all around them. They would learn that a woman's menstrual cycle linked her to the phases of the moon and the oceans; that the stars came out when the sun set, that a man's penis got hard when he looked at the shapely bodies of the female members of his tribe, and that woman gave birth to new life – the greatest miracle of all.

The ancient peoples saw the female form of the goddess reflected in the landscape, echoes of her recumbent form breathing life into the fertile soil. Women's mysteries were thought sacred – and menstrual blood was seen as a magical property. Shamanic priestesses would lead group sex rituals in which the whole community participated, sharing the ecstatic union of man and woman; woman and nature.

Whenever you feel jaded, try to effect similar thinking patterns to your ancestral sisters. Appreciate the changing seasons and ally yourself with nature, harmonizing with her rhythms and becoming the original earth goddess. Keep an eye on the phases of the moon and make a record of your arousal levels and how they work in tandem with the lunar cycle. Reflect on the phenomenal experience of being alive, with all the many natural wonders surrounding you.

* Take pleasure in being outdoors and visit the wild woodland at the time of changing seasons. This is very energizing and will connect you to the earth.

* Enjoy the sensual experience of fabrics that make your skin feel good and enjoy the healthy glow that comes after exercising.

✳ At least twice a year, make love outdoors – the most potent times being May Eve (30 April) or Winter Solstice (21 December) – bringing your senses alive as you feel and smell the earth beneath you.

✳ Look for sensual, female shapes in the landscape and enjoy a more earthy experience as you tap into your primal desires.

✳ When making love, relish each other's individual scent and tap into the primal energy and sexy synchronicity that has brought you together as a couple. When your lover enters you, you should look into each other's eyes, both breathing deeply into your lower abdomen and sex organs, allowing that most ancient of rites to take place. Your man's expression should be one of joy, as he is allowed the honour of the most intimate worship: that of orgasm in the presence of a goddess – you!

ancient egypt

Ancient Egypt was the first society to freely allow sexual diversity among its ruling class. Not only gay lifestyles flourished, but also cross-dressing and exhibitionism. Women were equal to men in Egyptian society, owning property and initiating divorce. Egyptian women loved dressing up and used elaborate cosmetics, flowers and ornaments to make themselves appear more like the goddesses. They invented kohl eyeliner and tattoos and made brightly coloured eye-shadows from natural resources.

The Egyptians performed unique and bizarre religious customs – often based upon the highly imaginative mythology of their gods and goddesses – incorporating strong sexual elements where women were the handmaidens of the gods' pleasure. Their wall paintings featured graphic genitalia, including even the clitoris. The temples were often used for rites of sexual pleasure where 'sacred prostitutes' would hold court. Masturbation was seen as a sacred rite – a direct copy of the god Amun giving birth to the world through the seed of his orgasm. A woman could go to the temple and perform sexual acts with whomever she pleased and exposing genitalia was encouraged in the temples.

Egyptian mythology tells of Osiris being hacked to pieces by his brother Seth. The great goddess Isis puts him back together but cannot find his phallus, so she creates a new one. Ancient Egyptians celebrated this event, during which women paraded through the streets with puppets displaying extremely large penises. But it is the mysterious Isis whose cult flourished, spreading north to Rome and even Britain, where the River Thames was originally known as Isis.

The Ancient Egyptians loved sensual adornment and beautification and saw the handling and worship of genitalia as sacred. And indeed it is! What other part of our bodies is as sensitive, responsive and impressive as our sexual centre?

✱ Set time aside to make a ritual out of giving yourself and each other genital worship.

✱ Get to know your own sexual anatomy. Study it and note its colours and folds without feeling ashamed. It's yours and you can do what you like with it.

✱ Give yourself permission to indulge in pleasure. When you take your partner's erection in your hand, get up close to it and worship it with your mouth and tongue as if you were performing a secret sexual initiation.

✱ Learn to love exposing yourself – but not in public! Men respond very quickly to the sight of female genitals and will be enflamed with desire by your confidence in giving him permission to explore without embarrassment. Look into his eyes with a smouldering expression as you reveal your most intimate self. Practise mutual masturbation. As he watches you touch yourself, he will become increasingly excited, which will further excite you as you build a repeating pattern of lust. Watch your partner enjoy himself and experiment by allowing him to ejaculate over your breasts. Think of him as being an ancient Egyptian god and offering you the tribute of his sacred seed. Similarly, you can orgasm into his face as he stimulates you orally.

✱ Be like the Egyptian women: decorate your eyes to effect a seductive look.

ancient greece

The modern West's understanding of the erotic begins with the Greeks, and their highly sophisticated culture was resplendent with gods and goddesses who seemed to represent little other than various facets of pleasure. The word 'erotic' itself originates from Eros, their mischievous boy-god of love. His female counterpart was the beautiful and flighty Aphrodite. Lesser-known goddesses such as Minerva, Athene and Cybele were adored as Wisdom, or Light, whilst Ceres represented fertility. The cult of Dionysus prevailed and the ceremonies performed in his honour were notorious for their shameless self-abandonment.

Much of the art of ancient Greece depicts satyrs and also the maenads – female followers of the love god – frolicking and fornicating. It was commonplace to have explicit decorations on household pottery. Penile wind chimes and water bowls were favoured artefacts, and a huge tumescent member was recognized as a good-luck charm.

The ancient Greeks were fond of secret rites, and at the core of their practice was their worship of the animal aspect of nature in man – in other words, they celebrated feeling horny. Although women were accorded few privileges under Greek law, the hetaerae – a higher echelon of courtesans – were sought out for their beauty, intelligence and wit, and could climb the social ladder as favoured lovers of political leaders. Houses of pleasure flourished but the shrewd hetaerae never forgot to pay homage to their mythical figurehead, Aphrodite, to whom many temples were dedicated.

The spirit of Dionysus – or Bacchus – is represented in the casting off of inhibitions. Always seeking the ecstatic experience, a devotee of Dionysus will embrace the explicitly sexual and seek to effect an altered state of consciousness through maximum arousal. For the past few decades this spirit has been evident in the erotic adoration of male pop stars, where young women will scream, dance or fantasize themselves into a frenzy of adoration of their god-like object of worship. Although your partner may not be a rock and roll sex idol, you can still take your sex life to a higher level of intensity by letting go of any inhibitions you have about exploring the full power of your sexuality.

✱ Try to get as relaxed as possible and don't allow any outside interference to penetrate your own little temple of lust.

✳ Allow yourselves to be decadent, taking turns to arouse each other with one-minute displays of eroticism, working toward two-minute turns of hands-on manipulation, each time being more daring.

✳ Try to imagine yourselves at an ancient Greek orgy, where no one was embarrassed about nakedness or erotic desires.

✳ Give something new a try, and see what feels thrillingly naughty and adventurous. Try inserting anal beads or letting your lover watch you use a vibrator – or, for the more authentic Greek experience, maybe he would like to play 'bend over, boyfriend' and experience the sensation of a slim dildo stimulating his anus. Take it slowly and gently, and use plenty of lubrication if this is his first time.

ancient rome

Synonymous with hedonism in all its forms, the Roman Empire was a society of sybarites. The decadent indulgence of the period included orgies, feasts, bathing parties and lewd games as entertainment, and saw the invention of an array of potions, perfumes, erotic artworks and the use of aphrodisiac foods. Asparagus, carrots, figs, nuts and oysters were plentiful at Roman feasts, but, for an exclusive turn-on, the sweat of gladiators was incorporated into wealthy women's massage potions. More pleasantly, roses were widely used. Ubiquitous in Roman mythology, the rose was seen as 'the nymph of flowers' and decorated ceremonial occasions as well as being used to stuff pillows and perfume public bath houses.

Their great goddess was, of course, Venus, the Lady of Love. Temples dedicated to Venus were schools of instruction in sexual technique, and came under the tutelage of a 'harlot priestess', who taught a spiritual approach to sex, similar to the Tantrism of the east. Venus the planet is also the Evening Star – the Stella Maris (Star of the Sea) – and an eternal link is formed between Venus and the oceans and heavens, making her the Celestial Mistress. Venus went on to become the muse of classical sculptors and Renaissance painters, and her name is still invoked today whenever we want a short-cut reference to matters of love.

Become skilled in the 'Venusian' arts. Although you won't be organizing an orgy, you can turn your living space into a modern-day temple of Venus by clearing away clutter and setting a scene fit for seduction.

✱ The imagination we brought to our playtime as children can still be used now we are adults. You can pretend to be the Emperor's consort. Indulge yourself in an extended session of bathing and grooming and find something sheer and flowing to wear. Use a rose-based essence in an oil burner and prepare a selection of aphrodisiac finger foods in small bowls that can be accessed from a reclining position. This is no time for shyness, but luckily emperors have total authority, so be prepared to be told what he wants you to do, as you will be performing special favours.

✱ Spread the floor with cushions, light scores of tea lights and candles, pour a bottle of red wine into an earthen pitcher with goblets, and get ready for fun.

✱ For this one night your partner will be treated to a sensual feast, but it is you who will be doing the indulging, immersing yourself in the role of a harlot priestess where you can be as teasing, seductive and wanton as you've always wanted to be. Fantasy role-play can enhance relationships and bring you closer together as a couple. When we share 'play', we bond in pleasure, which can bring joy into our lives. Feed him grapes and figs, massage him and dance for him.

✱ Same time next month, it's *his* turn to treat you, as you play the Empress and he your favourite servant.

imperial china & japan

Early Chinese and Japanese literature use naturalistic metaphors when referring to sexual acts and body parts. They didn't have gods and goddesses, but they were very nature-aware in terms of sexual metaphor. 'Jade gates' and 'unbending reeds' are easily decipherable, but 'clouds' and 'rain' were used to allude to vaginal moisture and semen.

The Taoist theory of yin and yang has survived many centuries and dynasties, but that famous balance of energies was applied in the ancient Chinese sexual doctrine to divide the distinct opposites of male and female. Women were thought to have an unlimited supply of yin, yet men had an easily exhaustible yang reserve. Consequently, it was regarded as unseemly for a man to use up his yang too quickly, especially in the wasteful art of self-pleasure. Before a man was allowed to ejaculate, he had to make a woman orgasm several times, producing many 'clouds' before his 'rain' could fall! In contrast, women were allowed to masturbate freely, as they suffered no loss of yin.

The Taoist culture flourished until the conservative Confucianist dynasty arrived in 221 BC, placing women in an inferior position to men, giving birth to the age of the concubine. When the Han dynasty arrived in the first century AD, the Taoist philosophies returned and sexual texts or 'pillow books' began to surface. These were the world's first sex manuals, and carried instructions for sexual positions as complicated and elaborate as anything found in the Kama Sutra.

In Taoism and Tantrism, great emphasis is put on sensual touching and kissing, because foreplay is seen as an essential part of lovemaking. The woman's vital juices need to be present before intercourse, as the sexual act needs to be an exchange of both yin and yang energy. A woman's yin energy or ch'i is receptive, and needs regular 'recharging' from a man's more active yang energy. Without regular harmonizing through sharing each other's unique essences, women can become sluggish and men can be irritable.

✷ Intercourse should not always involve male ejaculation. He should build his 'ching' (or semen) through practising a little restraint. Through so doing, according to Taoism, he will be much more 'manly' for it.

✱ Try out the ultimate Taoist sexual experience: set aside a day where you have penetrative sex five times. Each time, you must be brought to orgasm. It is more beneficial if your lover inserts his penis just before you climax, so he can absorb your essence. Then, only during the fifth 'session', will your man be allowed to ejaculate. It's a real test of his will!

✱ Change your attitude to lovemaking – see it not as a 'romantic' pursuit in the Western sense, but as a way of generating good health. When we are fully aroused, we experience a powerful flow of energy. Focus on that and make a mental record of how good it feels. That post-orgasmic endorphin rush is nature's great legal high, and its side effects are all good, such as boosting the immune system.

kama sutra

When we think of the Kama Sutra, myriad adventurous lovemaking positions spring to mind, but this is only one aspect of the ancient Indian Tantric practice of sacred sexuality that was first written down in the second century AD. If you want truly mind-blowing sex, then this philosophy of eroticism and spirituality is the best way to find sensual nirvana.

The main principle of the Kama Sutra is interconnectedness – the link between ourselves and the universe, body, mind and spirit. If this sounds a little too hifalutin, don't worry, because it's all about perfecting your sexual performance through experiencing as much pleasure as possible. You just have to remember to regard sex as sacred – a fine art.

In Hindu philosophy, female sensuality is recognized as an essential part of divinity. The Kama Sutra was not intended to be lewd. It was written with the serious intention of acquainting people with everything they needed to give their partner ultimate pleasure. Kundalini energy – represented by the female 'force' Shakti – is the deep-seated creative/erotic energy that smoulders within us all and uncoils like a snake when sexual feelings emerge. The divine conjunction of the lingam (penis) with the yoni (vagina) should bring about a state of bliss. No culture has so beautifully realized the visual and spiritual aspect of erotic love as Indian Tantrism. It is rich and colourful, and the world's most beautiful temples, such as that in Khajuraho, have been carved in the honour of its goddesses, such as Shiva's voluptuous consort, Parvati.

The Kama Sutra originated in a world where things moved slowly, but we need its harmonizing philosophy even more in our stressful modern times. Quality not quantity is the key to making love Kama Sutra-style. There is little in today's hectic lifestyle to nurture the spirit, and making time for quality one-on-one recreation is a great way to claw back the soulful experiences we all need.

✱ Discuss with your partner the idea of approaching sex from a more spiritual perspective. Talk to each other about what happens when you become aroused. Remember: the force that gives him an erection and makes you ready to receive it is about more than just physiology; you are invoking the timeless, universal kundalini energy.

✻ Indulge in the delights of seduction, making your room aesthetically conducive to eroticism. Clear clutter, hide away soft toys and odd socks, dim the lights and introduce a subtle display of fresh flowers or tealights. A furry animal-print bedspread is a fun touch, plus a few pillows and cushions to raise your hips for those adventurous positions!

✻ Work gradually towards intercourse as the crescendo of the event. Your arousal levels should build, so that, by the time you are ready for lingam/yoni contact, you have lost all inhibitions.

✻ If your man is sceptical about the spiritual side of sex, you will soon relax him into a sensual mood by offering a massage – men love them and never turn them down! Apply a warm, oiled palm to his sacrum – the small of his back, just above the tailbone. Gently rock and rub, and he will soon be putty in your hands.

courtly love
in the middle ages

Courtly love flourished in palaces and castles across France and England in the
Middle Ages, and was modelled on the feudal relationship between a knight and
his liege lord. A knight would fall passionately in love with a lady of higher rank,
whom he was meant to serve with unswerving loyalty. The lady in question was
almost always tantalizingly unavailable, and usually married, although marriages
back then were arranged on the basis of property and political advantage rather
than love. A lady was in complete control of a knight's affections, while the
knight was required to demonstrate obedience and submission as a lowly
servant. She would inspire him to do great deeds, often heroic and dangerous,
for which he would be rewarded with some minor gesture of approval.

Couples engaged in courtly relationships would exchange gifts and tokens and
ladies were wooed to the elaborate conventions of etiquette. No self-respecting
Rosamund or Eleanor could be seen making the sport of love too obvious, as
reputation was everything. Therefore, a bewimpled young lady would make the
most out of the power imbalance, enjoying her exhalted status as a dominant
goddess whilst her long-suffering admirer waited months, years, and sometimes
in vain, for his love to be consummated.

There is great reward to be had in delaying sexual gratification. Women, on the whole, are more skilled at playing the waiting game, especially in matters of lust, as they know they hold all the cards. A woman will relish putting a man through his paces, savouring every moment his attentions are focused on her, keeping him guessing as to whether all the effort will be worth his while. In our modern age of the 'want it now' culture, we have lost something of the art of courtship, so it can be great fun to encourage your man to revisit the old-fashioned sport of wooing.

✱ Instead of providing 'on-tap' sexual access, for one day try getting him to work at winning your favours and watch as he goes to great lengths to do so.

✱ Tell him you expect to see some effort, as what waits at the end of his pursuit will set him on fire, but he has to earn your womanly delights through a little hard work. He can journey out on a knightly crusade to bring you your favourite breakfast in bed, for instance.

✱ Or you might want to see a poem that expresses his amorous thoughts about you. If putting pen to paper seems too taxing, you can ask him to send you his lustful and affectionate billet-doux as an email or text expressing his desire. You will initially need to effect a haughty demeanour, but – to be fair to your noble lord – grant him reward where it is due as he proves his loyalty.

the age of the enlightenment

The Restoration of the 'merry' monarch Charles II in England in 1660 brought with it an era of relaxed moral attitudes. The burgeoning theories of Enlightenment scholars found swift favour with a nation that had not seen much fun under Puritan rule, where even dancing was banned.

By the 18th century, earthly pleasure was suddenly seen as healthy. Physicians prescribed lovemaking as a remedy for psychosomatic illnesses. This was also the time of rapid advancement in literary publishing and the erotic novel burst onto the scene, although circulation was limited to gentlemen of rank and means.

There was a flurry of economic expansion where new wealth was created fast from an expanding British Empire. London had as many brothels in the 1770s as it has coffee bars today. Secret societies flourished and ladies of a liberal disposition would be invited to attend gentlemen's clubs and salons, where fancy-dress parties were all the rage. Particularly popular were figures from classical mythology. Secret society parties were notorious for degenerating into drunken orgies not dissimilar to those of the ancient world. Gardens were landscaped to represent mythical idylls and a pagan sensibility crept back into fashion in the form of bawdy revelry and outdoor coupling. Rustic, ritual calendar customs began to be observed, such as dancing around the maypole – a representation of male virility and female fertility that harked back to pre-Christian times.

18th-century sex was earthy, and took inspiration from the pagan practices of the ancient world, especially Greece and Rome. In the 18th and 19th centuries it was customary for young people of country villages to make love in the woods on Mayday.

✱ If you have access to secluded parkland or woods in the springtime, have your man chase and capture you, resulting in doing what comes naturally. Your bawdy revelry will be a way of honouring the earth goddess and the old nature spirits.

✱ You can have a lot of fun playing the lady and the rake. Wear a push-up bra, low-cut, gypsy-style top and long skirt, and you can easily take on the appearance and attitude of the country wench. An oversized white shirt tucked into tight black pants will make your man look the part of the devilishly handsome young rogue.

✱ Gentlemen and ladies of the 18th century were very fond of cards, and wagers would be gambled on who lost their clothes first. Imagine yourselves to be lusty libertines, for whom down-and-dirty conversation is a prelude to naughty sport. Indulge in a little strip poker, undressing each other when an item of clothing is lost. You can go on to play for favours, such as oral fun or reading aloud the dirty bits of erotic novels. At the climax of the game, the decisive loser has to take a spanking, bent over the knee of the victor. Use a flat palm with an upward motion, making contact on the underside of the buttocks with your fingers. If your man is on the receiving end, so much the better!

MODERN BEDROOM GODDESS

how to be a modern goddess

A goddess cannot have low self-esteem! We need to approach love, sex and relationships with an open heart ... and a few tricks up our sleeves. Don't fall into the spiral of worrying unduly about your security within a relationship, fearful that the latest attractive woman to enter your social group is a threat. To warrant the treatment of a goddess, you need to act like someone who is worthy of worship in all weathers, who isn't going to resort to displaying signs of insecurity or jealousy at the merest hint of a glamorous distraction. The trainee goddess must learn to cultivate consistency of mood, generosity of spirit and an air of mystery. She must be a consummate professional in the art of seduction, thinking of herself as fabulous at all times. She will love flirting and entertaining and will know that men love women who listen to them.

The stresses of modern life can bring a goddess down! Sexual magnetism radiates outwards, and no number of designer clothes and upmarket cosmetics will compensate for a stressed-out body or soul. The modern goddess needs to be healthy, to stimulate energy through her body. The contribution that our lifestyles make to our overall zest levels affects our libido more than anything else does. The best way to remain in peak condition is to be a warrior for your own cause and ensure you get enough light, movement, hydration, nourishment and tranquillity.

modern goddess lifestyle plan

LIGHT Be outdoors for at least one hour every day. Walk in the park, borrow a dog, go for a cycle ride, do some gardening. Make sure your face is in the light. Remember how good you feel when you are on holiday? This is as much to do with the amount of time you spend outdoors as it is having a break from routine.

MOVEMENT Our bodies haven't changed since the days we were hunters and nomads, but modern life involves a lot of sitting, where the precious life force stagnates. This can cause everything from depression to obesity. Try dance, yoga, Pilates or any of the Eastern body disciplines. Your improved posture will get you noticed – very useful for flirting with someone sexy.

NUTRITION A goddess needs to be careful what she puts into the temple of her body. Mechanically processed foods high in fat and salt will suppress the libido. Resist the fast-food chains – they contribute nothing to our wellbeing.

HYDRATION Drink two litres of water a day. Dehydration causes depression and even organ malfunction, especially if combined with high levels of alcohol consumption. This doesn't mean you have to go on a 'detox'. Drinking more water will do the same job.

TRANQUILLITY Be still for a few moments of reflection each day. This will help you achieve a calmer disposition and be receptive to the positive energy of sexual attention. Try breath work. Imagine that each in- breath is full of golden, healing 'particles'. As you breathe out, visualize the dull particles of stress leaving your body.

intuition & flirting

Women have inbuilt finely tuned receivers that pick up on the slightest signal of a man's erotic interest in them, or in one of their female friends. Surprisingly the spoken word accounts for less than ten per cent of how we form opinions of each other. Human communication is reliant on a mass of subtle factors. When two potential lovers strike up a conversation, messages start firing at an unconscious level, determining whether or not they find each other attractive. The olfactory sense plays a bigger part than spoken language, which is why we shouldn't drench our natural scent with man-made perfumes and sprays. A man should be able to smell perfume only when leaning in for a kiss; and not be able to smell it from a metre's distance.

Sexual tension is the best aphrodisiac, and stringing out the flirtatious stage can be exquisite torture! Throughout history, courtesans found their way into the male domain, where they made a fine art out of flirting. It is a wise woman who knows that men find an intellectual equal a great tonic to the libido. Contrary to the narrow-minded opinion that men have one-track minds, they do not necessarily prefer model looks over intelligence and a sharp wit. The modern goddess should study psychology, read up on current affairs, learn about art, music and literature, and form her own opinions.

If you have an unusual hobby or pastime, talking about it can pique the interest of a successful and desirable man. A lot of men find active women incredibly sexy. You will have more to talk about in social gatherings, and this will earn you the flattering male attention that we all love!

The bedroom goddess will know the decisive moment when it is make or break time and, if he doesn't lean in for the kiss, then she will have to. The person who makes the first move is always the one who directs how the sex will pan out – soft and gentle, down and dirty, or high-energy and playful. It's your call – just be brave and go for it!

✱ Act as if you have the juiciest secret and you will only reveal it if he gets really close.

✱ Listen to what he says rather than worrying about what you look like.

✱ Make sure you have fresh breath and luscious lips – not war-paint lipstick, but neutral and glossy.

✱ Practise walking just that little bit more sexily in front of him.

✱ Have opinions – even if they conflict with his. This will open up debate, which is good for building erotic tension.

✱ Let your hair swing as you walk. If it's short, run your hands through it a couple of times when talking to him – be careful not to look too obvious, though!

✱ Be tactile: stroke things, toy with things, become more obviously sensual.

✱ Don't be afraid to move in really close to him, but without touching. This can drive him wild, so watch out for a sudden movement as a reflex reaction.

✱ Tease him. If you know his name, start calling him Mr whoever. The sudden formality will act as an erotic jolt.

lingerie & rituals

Sexual energy is the most powerful energy we can harness for bringing love and pleasure to our relationships. The golden rule is not to rush into dressing for pleasure. Make an erotic ritual out of it. Performing rituals is a way of making everyday acts a bit more special, tapping into the rich inner world of the true self. In our private lives, ritual can be as simple as lighting a candle or incense in our bedroom – to 'set the scene' – or using a particular pillow in lovemaking. Once we have enacted a preparation ritual, we can feel more easily entitled to our own sacred space of sexual pleasure.

Generally, men do not dress for sex. Putting on the sensual garments of seduction is something only women do. The female form – whatever its size – is enhanced to best effect with the aid of decorative underwear. Lingerie is the final frontier before the main event, and is what stands between a man's touch and your full-on naked intimacy. Most men have definite opinions about their lingerie preferences: from thrillingly naughty and sheer, to expensive, satin and French.

Sexy underwear is only as effective as the woman wearing it – and this is where confidence is essential. The bedroom goddess needs to project an alluring aura of promise. The act of displaying your assets to their best advantage will fire your man's visual receptors straight to his erogenous zones. Women love showing off to an appreciative audience and men love voluptuous eye candy. It's a perfect match!

In ancient Babylonia, joy maidens or ishtaritu groomed themselves to perfection, revelling in their femininity to bring about the life-enhancing energy of sexual union. When you create your own sacred space for sex magic – this will make each meeting with your partner special.

✱ Find out your man's favourite style of underwear. After bathing and anointing yourself with your most exotic body lotion, ease into your chosen lingerie, knowing that this procedure is wholly feminine and that its effect will render you heart-stoppingly gorgeous.

✱ The next time you slip into your smalls, indulge yourself in the ritual of dressing up, taking time to ease on sheer, shiny stockings or cute frilled gingham panties. Observe how feminine the garments feel on your body.

✻ Don't just lie on the bed and wait for him; put on some high heels and walk seductively around the room.

✻ Try catching him unawares in the kitchen, when you are both standing up. Sex play is usually better if it starts from a standing position, as there is more dynamism to your body energy. If you walk around him in heels and his favourite lingerie whilst he is fully clothed, he will not be able to resist you and he will do anything to get his hands on you.

✻ Tease him, and don't yield to him straight away. Remember that men love to chase! By performing this age-old ritual of erotic dressing, you can imagine yourself to be a skilled courtesan in your own pleasure palace!

fun-loving seduction

We always think of seduction as what we do to make ourselves desirable to men – the decoration, the clothes, the make-up – but the vast majority of women stop short of initiating actual sex. Men like to please, impress and entertain women, but similarly it makes a wonderful change for them when a woman takes the lead.

Most men are just waiting for that rare encounter when they don't have to shoulder all the responsibility for the adult event. Also, it is marvellously thrilling to hear yourself saying the things that we traditionally leave to men, such as verbally expressing how aroused you are, how you cannot wait to take him to bed. It's a real adrenaline rush to be the complete seductress.

A lot of women refrain from making instrumental moves because they think it will make them look easy or sluttish. If a man has such repressed ideas about courtship – enough to be put off by the adult advances of a gorgeous woman – then he will be too much hard work anyway. If you approach your subject with subtlety and grace – rather than loud and drunkenly! – you are bound to elicit a positive response. An attractive person making an effort to seduce you can be a great boost for your sense of self-worth, as most women know, so wouldn't it be fun to flatter the male ego for once and take the reins yourself!

taking the lead

If you have gone some way down the road of flirtation, why not take things further and play the part of the true seductress? Our intuition tells us when mutual attraction is working because we can feel the sexual energy bouncing between the desired man and ourselves.

Men love to hear women talk about sex because female arousal is one of the great mysteries and it's something they're forever trying to figure out. You can steer the conversation to your favourite sex scene in a movie, or tell him what book turned you on the most and why. Then you can ask for his and, whatever he tells you, you can playfully say how naughty he is! Also, you'll have got a sneaky insight into the workings of his sexual mind.

Move up closer to him and angle in for a kiss, caress his upper body, and don't rush 'downstairs'. Keep the atmosphere playful and unhurried – this will put him at ease. His erection won't disappear the instant you stop touching him! Try running both hands up his thighs and smiling at him. You'll get an amazing buzz when you see how much he's enjoying your advances. Throw him some compliments about his appearance during the 'hands-on' stage, and you'll be an accomplished seductress in no time!

a little domination

Like the courtesans of ancient civilizations, the sexually dominant woman should be skilled in the art of psychological power-play, knowing how to tease and drive a man wild. One way to incorporate a little domination into your sex life is to play body worship.

Both sit fully dressed facing each other, but you should wear something that makes you feel invincible: hold-ups and high heels with a formal white shirt and dark skirt should do the trick. It's useful to have something to hold – a feather is good, if you don't own a riding crop, but you should toy with it menacingly as if it were an instrument of correction. It's important for you to keep a straight face and you have to look as if you are in control, as laughter can break the erotic charge. Ask him to confess something personal to you, such as when he last masturbated (all men do!) and what he thought about when he was doing it. Ask him to be specific with the details, remembering to effect the expression of a stern matron. He should call you 'mistress' or 'Miss' (whatever you surname is). You can make him crawl to you for forgiveness for his filthy ways and plant kisses on your shoes and your legs. His reward will be to worship you, bringing you to orgasm with his mouth.

sexual technique

The modern goddess will be a good observer and listener, naturally sensitive to the desires of her partner and completely tuned to her own. She will recognize that all men depend on women for comfort, love and sex, and to hold that power is a privilege that should be used compassionately.

As a goddess you are part of the eternal continuum of romance and flirtation that has existed since the beginnings of humankind. Each pairing of individuals produces a unique 'dance'. Although we each have preferred styles of lovemaking, the experience still manages to be completely different with each love match.

The first three months of a relationship is when partners find their lovemaking pattern – a time of wild energy and excitement, when you cannot keep your hands off each other. Many sex manuals explain how best to pleasure each other and describe a variety of sexual positions, but you cannot go wrong by knowing the following: all men love to feel something warm, moist and snug around their penis and, after ejaculating, men generally cannot help falling asleep. So do try to have your orgasm before his, to avoid disappointment and remember sex is a process of give and take.

loving yourself
as a goddess

Sex is always more rewarding when it is undertaken with enthusiasm and joy, and there is no better way to do this than to unite sex with spirit. By enhancing your love life with some of the techniques and philosophies of ancient, goddess-aware cultures, you can tap into truths and revelations that may change your world-view.

Never accept mediocre sex when you could be taking your pleasure to higher levels. By following the five points of the Modern Goddess Lifestyle Plan (see pages 48–49), you will be nourishing both body and soul. Take your lovers with you on your journey – men are more vulnerable and sensitive than we readily assume, and it can be wonderfully enriching to explore a creative sexual life together.

By loving yourself and making the best of the body nature has given you, you will radiate confidence. When you are working in tandem with the universal energies, living the life you deserve and harnessing power through fulfilling sex, then you will know that the spirit of the goddess is within you!

index